Twenty Walks around Swindon

Originally published in 1991 as 'Thamesdown Rambles' by Borough of Thamesdown, Arts and Recreation, Parks and Landscape Division.

Revised and up-dated by The North East Wilts Group of The Ramblers' Association in 2000, 2003 and 2011

Production by Rob Dawson

Printed in England by Avon Printing Services
Roundponds, Melksham, SN12 8EB
01225 700303, avonprintingservices.com

Printed on paper produced from sustainable forests

ISBN 1-906494-59-2

Location of Walks

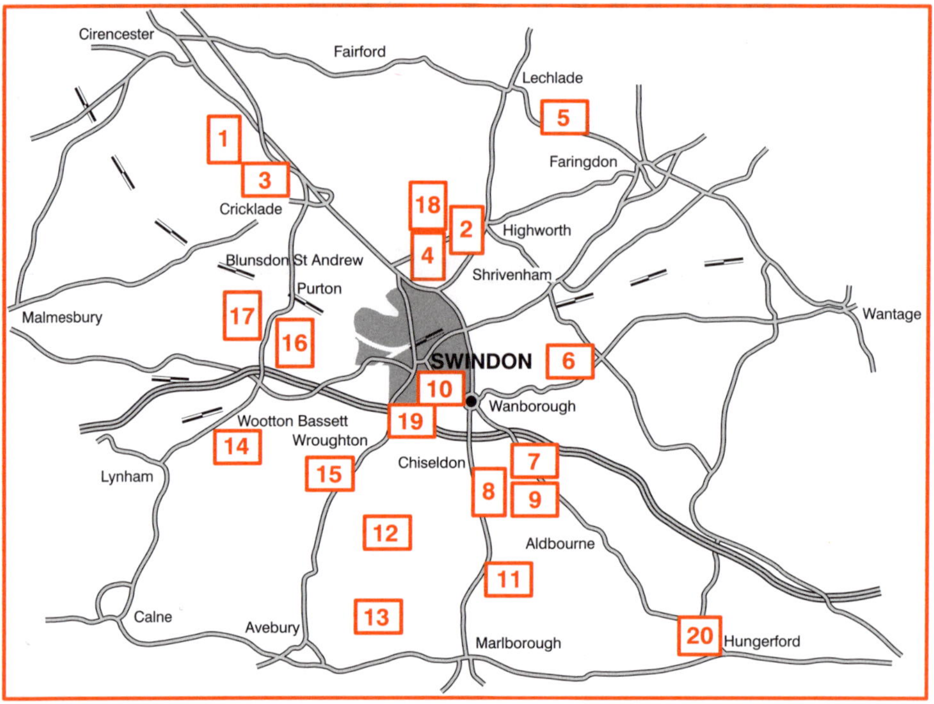

Ordnance Survey Maps

It is advisable to use Ordnance Survey maps in conjunction with the sketch maps in this book, but occasionally there will be a discrepancy between the two because of changes that have occurred on the ground and are not yet shown on the OS maps. The sketch maps attempt to show a route that is correct at the time of publication.

Ordnance Survey maps can be bought at local bookshops or borrowed from Marlborough and Swindon libraries.

Disclaimer

Every effort has been made to ensure the accuracy of the information in this booklet but The Ramblers cannot accept any responsibility for changes which affect the routes described or for the consequences.

If using public transport please remember that bus services change frequently. Check that the quoted bus service is still running before setting out.

Walks Index

Walk 1 Cotswold Water Park

Walks generally on good level tracks often close to lakes which have been formed as a result of gravel extraction, and alongside disused canal and railway. The path between points 1 and 3 is subject to flooding after prolonged wet weather.

Distance: 2 (A), 3½ (B) and 4½ (C) miles

OS Maps: Explorer 169 Landranger 163

Start: **Car:** Leave the A419, Swindon to Cirencester road at the Spine Road junction and go down Spine Road for 300 yards. Turn left into the car park. The Gateway Centre has a café, toilets and information leaflets.

Bus: No. 51 from Swindon *(no Sunday service)*.

Directions:

Walk A - 2 miles

1. With your back to the Gateway Centre, cross the car park aiming to go under the bridge *(built in 2004)* which carries Spine Road over the Thames & Severn Canal. Walk along the old tow path a short distance and at the next bridge go up the ramp to a kissing gate and finger post.
2. Take path to the left, signposted South Cerney 1½ miles, and continue to a metal gate with a kissing gate alongside. Pass through this and continue to the River Churn.
3. Cross the river by the smaller bridge and turn left, soon with views of a lake on the right. This reaches the forecourt of a sailing club. Continue straight forward to the road. Cross the road and river (slightly left) to a signed path to Cerney Wick. Continue on this path with the river on the right until coming to a concrete bridge; cross the river on this, over a stile and turn left. Follow the lake to its end and continue between the lake and the stream.
4. Turn left and follow the stream to another stile. Immediately over this turn left over a bridge - there is a gate here with steps for climbing over. Now keeping the lake on the left, follow the hedge to the corner.
5. Here there is a choice: turn left again to follow the lake back to the car park *(the building can be seen over the hedge)*; or find a bridge over the stream and through the hedge to turn left along the old canal and return to the car park.

Round House on the Thames & Severn Canal at Cerney Wick

Walk B – 3½ miles

1. Commence as walk A to the finger post above the bridge.
2. This time take the straight on route to South Cerney by going right through the gate and turning immediately left alongside the old Thames and Severn canal.

   ***(WARNING** Immediately over the fence is one of the old locks that is unfenced and quite deep. Take care with children.)*

   Follow this path through to a tarmacadam road with a footpath sign showing left to South Cerney ½ mile (straight ahead Siddington).

6. Turn left along this country lane. On coming to the outskirts of the village, look for a wooden footbridge to the left over a stream with two gates leading to a surfaced footpath. Follow this to reach the main road.

7 Turn left and follow the road to the edge of the village. As the road begins to curve right, look for a road marked Wildmoor Way on the left.

8. Follow this to the footpath sign 'Cerney Wick –1½ miles'.
3. On reaching a short concrete section of lane, take the signed path on the right that follows the side of the lakes until reaching the River Churn. Turn right just before the river, go alongside the lake and cross in front of the sailing club as walk A and follow that route via 4 and 5 to return to the car park.

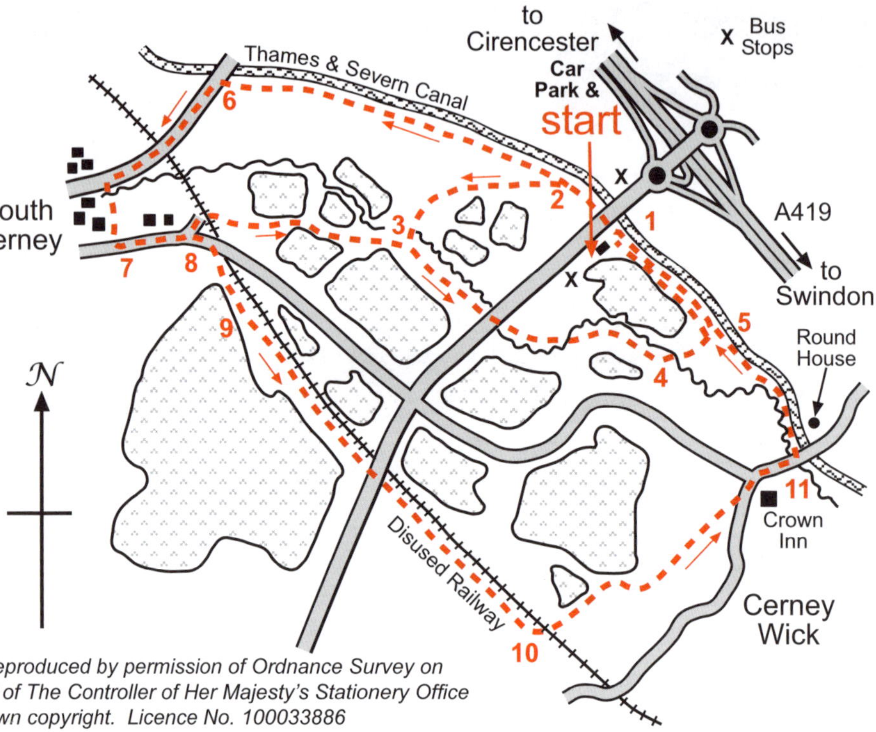

Map reproduced by permission of Ordnance Survey on behalf of The Controller of Her Majesty's Stationery Office

Walk C – 4½ miles

1. Follow the route as walk B round to the edge of the village at 8 but now follow the main road as it curves to the right, crossing the road to walk on a fenced cycle track (Route 45) beside the road.

9. Take this path through to the road at the viaduct. Cross the road and continue along the bridleway to a point where it broadens out with a signpost showing Cerney Wick 0.5 m.

10. Turn left through a gate and walk along a grass path with a lake away to the left. Cross a V-stile and bridge, go up steps and turn right to walk round the lake to reach a lane. Cross the lane and another stone stile to a road with the Crown Inn on the corner. Go straight ahead following the footpath sign 'South Cerney' and look for another sign pointing left to South Cerney along the line of the old canal.

11. Turn left and walk with the canal and lock on the right. Note the old lock keeper's round-house. Follow the footpath back to the car park or at 5 at the footpath sign 'River Churn' turn left to the lakeside and then right to find the car park.

Refreshments: Gateway Centre; Crown Inn, Cerney Wick (Walk C)

Highworth, Red Down & Hannington

Walk 2

An undulating walk through varied countryside with good views.

Distance: 6½ miles

OS Maps: Explorer 169 Landranger 173, 174

Start: **Car:** Car park in Brewery Street, Highworth, (SU203924). From Swindon, turn right at the roundabout on reaching Highworth; this is Brewery Street. The car park is along on the right.

Bus: No. 7 from Swindon.

Directions:

1. Turn left out of the car park and walk along Brewery Street to the A361. *(Notice Vorda Pre-school on the right; Vorda is supposed to be the Roman name for Highworth.)* Cross to the Fox Hotel and then use the pedestrian crossing to cross the A361. Go into The Green, pass The Rose and Crown, turn left to the Recreation Centre and go through the car park. Keeping the wall of the Centre on the right, go ahead to the playing field. Go diagonally across the field, keeping the children's swings and slide on the left. At the corner of the field cross a stile and turn left. Keeping the hedge on the left and the pitch and putt course on the right, follow the yellow markers through a gap in the hedge and to the bottom of the field.
2. Turn right for about 50 yards, then left through a gap in the hedge. Take the path going straight ahead, keeping to the right of oak trees. At the next hedgerow, go through the kissing gate and continue ahead. The hill in front is Red Down with Red Down Farm on the left. At the summit of the Down, with a line of tall trees on the left, go straight on to a gate in the hedge ahead. Turn right along a track and, after about 100 yards, in the corner of a field, turn left. Walk downhill with a hedge on the right to a gap, with finger post, about 100 yards before the bottom of the field.
3. Turn right. Continue with the hedge on the right and at the next field boundary go through a gap. Keep straight ahead as the path becomes a track and, at the next field boundary, bear right through a gateway. *Notice the line of ash trees on the left.* Follow the track with the hedgerow on the right to reach the road, B4019.
4. *The Freke Arms is just to the left.* From there take the road signposted Hannington and Castle Eaton. The road rises to cross the track of the

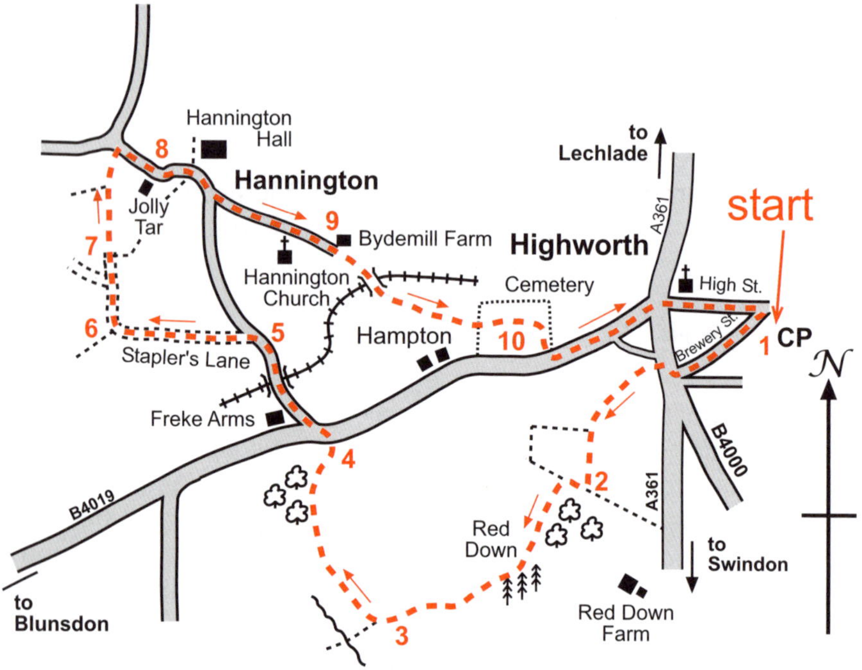

disused Highworth branch line (which was opened in 1883 and closed in 1953). At the top of the hill take the signposted bridleway going left.

5. *This is Stapler's Lane.* After about 200 yards, new fencing marks the line of the water pipeline from Farmoor Reservoir to Blunsdon Reservoir. After about ½ mile, where the track curves left and goes downhill at 6.

6. Turn right, slightly uphill, into another track. In about 300 yards, where a path goes over a stile near a gap, keep straight on. A short distance further on there is a gap and a track goes to the right. Still keep straight on and continue along a wide track to a finger post. Turn right down narrow track, keeping fence on the left. Go through kissing gate into field on the left.

7. Bear right across the field, keeping the bell tower of a chapel at Hannington straight ahead. Go through the kissing gate and make for another kissing gate to left of two bungalows, then walk between a bungalow and a hedge to the road. Turn right to the Jolly Tar Inn.

   On the wall in the bar is the nameplate of the locomotive "Hannington Hall" which was built at Swindon Railway Works in 1933.

8. Continue in the same direction, passing the entrance to Hannington

Hall on the left, to a grassy triangle where the road turns right. Keep straight ahead down a metalled track. *A good view of the Hall (built in 1653) is obtained by looking back about half way down the track. Hannington church is on the right.*

9. Go on down the road to Bydemill Farm and, after crossing the millstream, turn left. Pass through a kissing gate and bear left to go through a kissing gate and over a bridge over a stream. Continue in the same direction to a grassy bridge over the disused railway line (look left). Go on over the stile and continue straight on between wooden fences. Make for the top right corner of the field. Go through a small gate and follow a sunken track to the left of a garden. Cross the track, at Hampton, and go over a stone stile opposite. Keeping the bell tower of the cemetery chapel ahead, cross another stone stile and, bearing slightly left, make for a gate in the boundary wall of the cemetery. *Good views of Hannington Hall and Fairford airfield are obtained from here.*

10 Cross the cemetery by a concrete path, follow the path between garden fences then right on to the B4019. Turn left and walk to the traffic lights. Go across into High Street and down to the car park.

Refreshments: The Freke Arms
The Jolly Tar - Hannington
Highworth - various.

Hannington Church

Walk 3 Cricklade & Cotswold Water Park

*A level walk starting along a good track on a disused railway line and returning mostly beside a disused canal where the path is rougher in places but improves as the route enters the North Meadow Nature Reserve. However, North Meadow is often flooded in winter and the path between **11** and **12** can be impassable. If so, then cross the Thames at **11** and follow bridleway, rejoining route just south of **12**.*

Distance: 5½ and 2½ miles

OS Maps: Explorer 169 Landranger 163

Start: **Car:** Cricklade Leisure Centre (SU094937). The Centre is on the NW edge of Cricklade, signposted off the B4040, sometimes as "Sports Centre".

Bus: No. 51 stops in Calcutt Street *(no Sunday service)*.

Directions:

1. Leave the car park by a gravel path at the far end of the building, going to the left. After a short distance go under a bridge at **2** (see map)
2. This is the disused track of the Midland & South West Junction Railway *(that was opened in 1884 and closed in 1961)*. After about a mile cross the River Thames at **3**.
3. **SHORT WALK**: After a few yards, turn right, cross a stile, then follow the river downstream, joining the main walk at **11**. (See later)

   MAIN WALK: Continue along the railway path, passing under a high brick-arched bridge.
4. Continue, passing a stile and signpost on the right to Cerney Wick. Pass a further concrete stile on the right then look for some steps and a footbridge on the right, signposted Gateway Centre.
5. Leave the railway track here, crossing this footbridge and then three others. The path then becomes a narrow, fenced track. Continue on this track to reach a road.
6. Turn right and follow this winding road until just before you reach the Cerney Wick village sign.
7. Turn left over a footbridge, signed 'S. Cerney', bear right through the kissing gate, then left over a gated footbridge. Follow the path, with a hedge on the right and the lake on the left, to the far corner to find and cross a footbridge.
8. Turn right on to the canal towpath and follow this past a round house and lock on your left and then cross the road *(to your right is the Crown Inn)*.

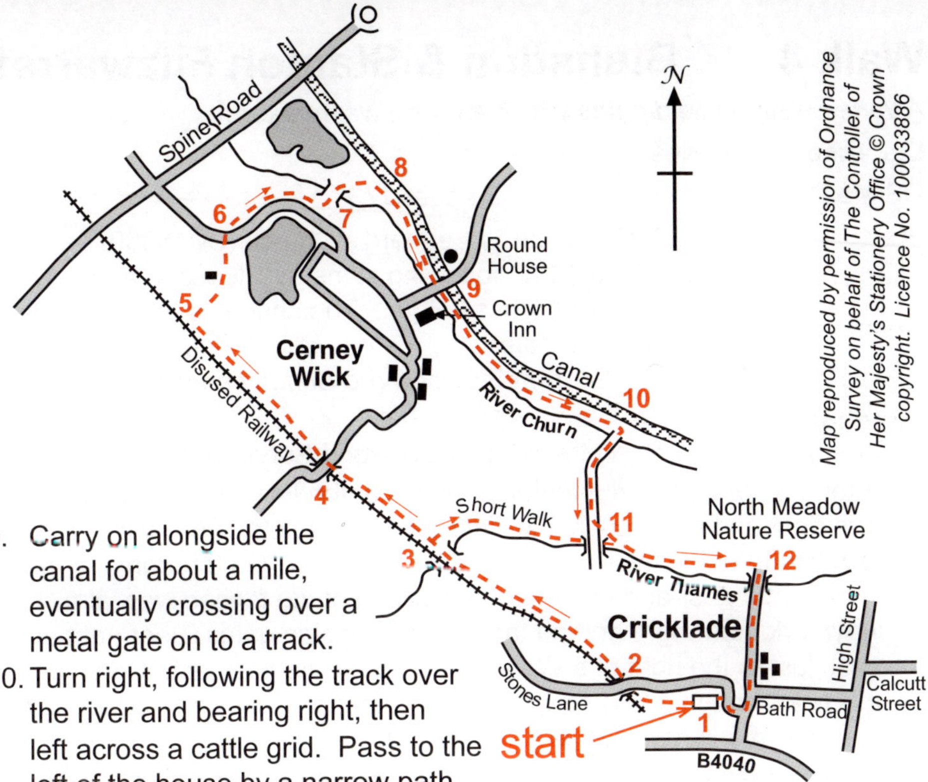

9. Carry on alongside the canal for about a mile, eventually crossing over a metal gate on to a track.
10. Turn right, following the track over the river and bearing right, then left across a cattle grid. Pass to the left of the house by a narrow path leading across a footbridge and on to the route of the North Wiltshire Canal *(which was opened in 1819)*. Follow the path via a footbridge to reach the bridge over the Thames at 11.
11. This is where the short walk rejoins. Turn left down steps to a gate before crossing the bridge, into the North Meadow Nature Reserve. *(This is an ancient meadow and is particularly noted for the spring-flowering snake's head fritillary.)* Follow the bank of the Thames until just after a flume and meter house when you reach a concrete bridge.
12. Cross the bridge, bear right and left into a lane. Continue forward when it joins Hallsfield, pass Reeds, then turn right into Stones Lane and back to the start.

Refreshments: Crown Inn at Cerney Wick
Pubs and shops in Cricklade

Public Transport Option:

Alight at Calcutt Street. Cross High Street with care by the clock tower and take narrow road opposite. Pass Jenner Hall, fire station and cemetery. At T-junction turn right. Follow sign to "Sports Centre" to start the walk. Additional distance ½ mile each way.

Walk 4 Blunsdon & Stanton Fitzwarren

A varied walk on field paths which are well waymarked.

Distance: 6 miles

OS Maps: Explorer 169 Landranger 173

Start: **Car:** At Blunsdon St Leonard's Church (SU153907). Turn off the A419, following signs for Blunsdon and, later, Blunsdon House Hotel. The church is about ½ mile after the hotel.

Bus: No. 24 from Swindon *(no Sunday service)*.

Directions:

1. Keeping the church on the left go east along Burytown Lane.
2. After the cemetery, at a footpath sign Stanton Fitzwarren 1½ miles, turn right and go through a kissing gate into a field. Follow the right-hand edge of the field to a second kissing gate. Go through and turn left along a post-and-rail fence. Near end of the fenced way, at a waymark, bear right and go through two kissing gates. Bear right and pass just to the right of a World War 2 gun emplacement. Continue on this line through a kissing gate to the road (B4019). Turn left along the road for 350 yards. (Beware fast traffic).
3. At the footpath sign, turn right through a kissing gate and follow the right hand edge of the field, then turn left along the far edge to reach a kissing gate. Follow the left edge of the field to a gate and bridge. Carry on up the left edge of the next field to another gate and stile on the left. Cross this stile and follow the field edge, keeping to the hedge on the right, for the next four fields. At the fifth field come out on the Mill Lane Track, follow signpost Kingsdown.
4. Walk beside woodland, then across a field to the track of the dismantled Swindon to Highworth railway. *(The railway opened in 1883 and the last train ran to Highworth in 1953.)* Follow the track with Great Wood on the left and, when it reaches a field, follow the right hand edge to Kingsdown Lane.
5. Turn left along Kingsdown Lane and, in about 300 yards, turn right through a kissing gate. Follow a wide track around the cemetery and come out on to Kingsdown Road near the crematorium entrance.
6. Turn right along the road for 200 yards and then turn right up a track, signpost 'Hyde Farm ½', that leads between an electricity sub-station and some industrial units. Follow the track round to the left, passing a mobile home park on the right. Go through a kissing gate and follow the track onward along the right hand edge of a field *(planted as part of*

Great Western Community Forest). On entering the next field turn to the right and follow the edge to the far right corner. Go through a gap in the fence and turn right, then follow the path behind Hyde Farm and the stored caravans.

7. After the stored caravans, turn half left and follow the path heading for a rusty corrugated iron building, behind a hedge, on the far side of the field. This will lead to a kissing gate between the hedge and the corner of a shed. Follow the path along the back of several sheds to regain Kingsdown Lane.
8. Cross the road and follow a house drive, signpost 'Broad Bush ½', keeping the hedge on the right. Carry on, keeping by this hedge, over three fields, through a kissing gate, over a footbridge, and through a second kissing gate in the far corner. Follow the path across the field to a kissing gate in the hedge opposite. Go through and follow the left hand edge up hill. Keep to the hedge and enter a narrow path which emerges on the road by a letterbox.
9. Turn left along the road. Just after Beech Lea, turn right on to a track, signposted as a footpath High Street ½ mile. At the end, with a bungalow on the right, turn left at the end of the cottages. Turn right on to a road and then left after the new houses. Go down the hill towards the Methodist Church and at the High Street turn right to return to the Church.

Refreshments: Heart in Hand, High Street, Blunsdon and Village Shop.

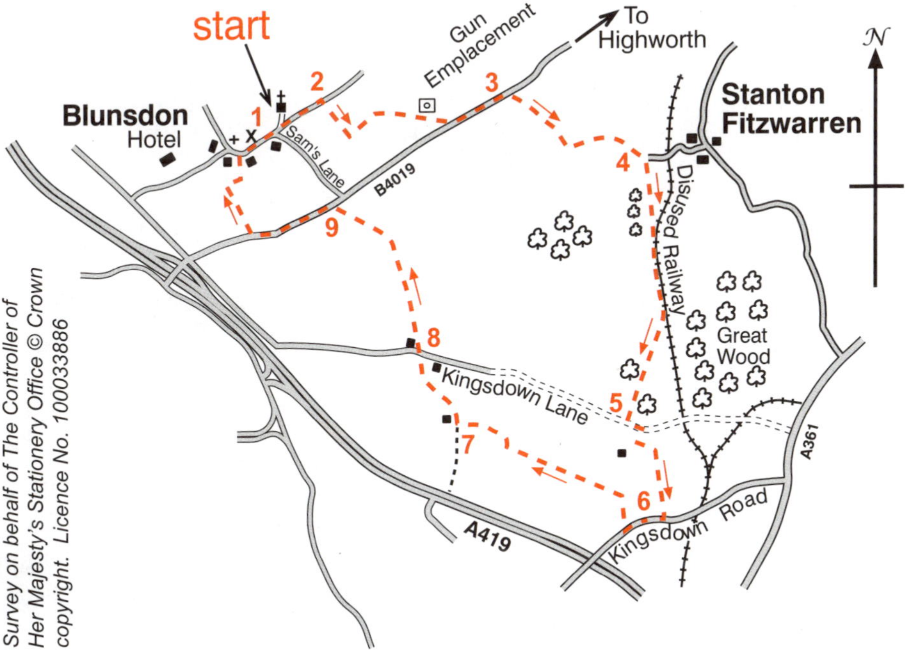

Map reproduced by permission of Ordnance Survey on behalf of The Controller of Her Majesty's Stationery Office © Crown copyright. Licence No. 100033886

10.10.13 (small variants)

Walk 5 Lechlade, Buscot & Kelmscot

A walk along the bank of the Thames and across fields.

Distance: Possible walks of 2, 4 and 6 miles by crossing the Thames at Points 2, 3 and 4 respectively. The complete walk will be 7½ miles

OS Maps: Explorer 170 Landranger 163

Start: **Car:** Park at the Riverside car park, Lechlade. (SU212992). Circuits can also be started from St. John's Lock, Buscot or Kelmscot.

Bus: Nos. 64 and 74 from Swindon *(infrequent service)*.

Directions:

1. From the car park, walk within the Country Park towards the bridge and cross the river. Continue into Lechlade, turning right at the road junction to reach the main square. Enter the churchyard and pass to the left of the Church entrance through the kissing gate and along the tarmac path to the main road (approx. ½ mile).
2. Cross the road and follow the minor road opposite, signposted 'Kelmscot'. At Leaze Farm dairy turn right into the entrance and follow the gravel path to its end, climb the stile on the right and turn left after 20 yards over two wooden bridges. Turn left and cross the field to reach a gap in the fence and continue to Buscot Lock.
3. At the lock cross the first weir only and turn half left to leave by a stile beyond the lock. Follow the bank and cross the concrete bridge. Turn right and follow the riverbank for just over a mile to a boat club and enter by a grey gate.
4. With the bridge on the right leave at gate exit, turning left. Keep the fence on the left. Cross the bridge over a stream and continue in the same direction but veer so that the hedge is on the right. At the end of the field, turn right on to a wide track and follow it into Kelmscot. At 'The Plough', turn right and walk through the village past Kelmscot Manor *(where William Morris lived)* until the river is reached. Follow the river (on the left) to the boat club.

Lechlade

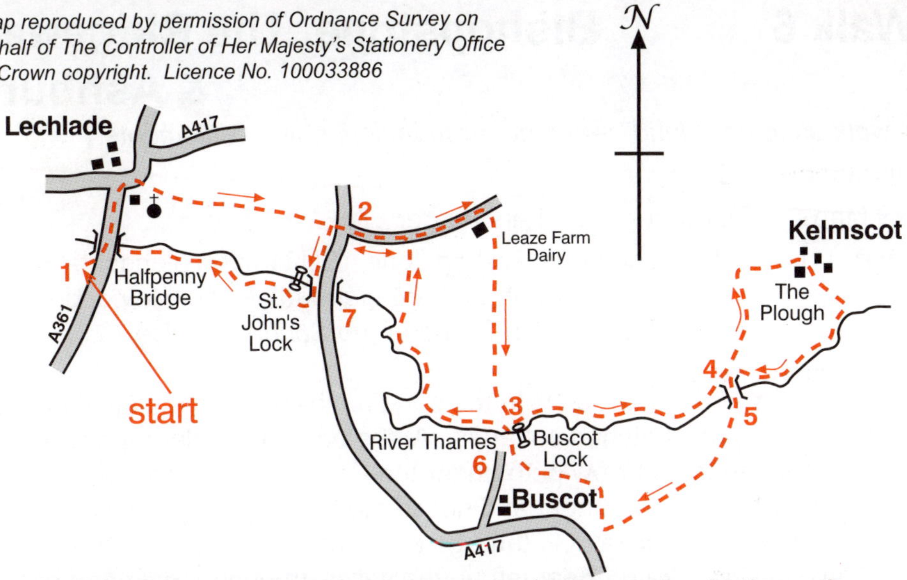

5. Cross the bridge and take the stile to the tarmac path. As the path bends to the left, turn half right, aiming for the left of two trees. Walk along hedgerow, keeping hedge on right, to a stile and bridge. Turn right and continue forward keeping the hedge on the right **(do NOT follow it round to the right)** to a bridge over a ditch 20 yards to the right at the next hedgeline. Turn half right to cross the next field to a marker and continue diagonally to the far corner of the field to reach a road at the corner. Immediately turn right and walk down the track, turning left at the 5-bar gate and follow the field edge. At the hedge gap, after an electricity pole, go to the other side of the hedge and follow it to a wooden bridge at the corner. Cross the field to the river lock.

6. Cross the lock and weir to a stile. Turn left and follow the riverbank to a 'squeeze' stile. Turn left to take the path under trees to reach a minor road. Turn left and turn left again at 'The Trout'. Cross the river and enter St. John's Lock by the grey gate on the right. *At the side of St. John's Lock is a fine statue of Old Father Thames that was originally sited at the source of the Thames.*

7. Pass through the lock and continue with the river on the right, eventually passing under Halfpenny Bridge at Lechlade to reach the start. *The halfpenny refers to the toll that was levied when it was a toll bridge. The old tollhouse is built into the northeast corner of the bridge.*

Refreshments: Pubs and cafes in Lechlade
'The Trout' at St. John's Bridge
'The Plough' at Kelmscot.

Walk 6 Bishopstone, The Ridgeway & Ashbury

A walk on to downland, returning through spring-line settlements.

Distance: 5½ miles

OS Maps: Explorer 170 Landranger 174

Start: **Car:** The pond, Bishopstone. (SU246837) alongside B4507 Wanborough to Wantage road. Roadside parking.
Bus: No. 90 from Swindon *(no Sunday service)*.

Directions:

1. Walk away from the road with the pond on the left to a metalled path on the left past thatched cottages. At the bend by a telegraph pole, turn right on to a narrow path under the eaves of cottages and left up steps to a drive. Turn right and notice the Iron Age strip lynchets on the hill in the distance. Go through a kissing gate and cross the field to a stile beside a gate. Bear left up the valley, through a gate and bear right. Climb to the signpost on the Ridgeway, with a reservoir on the skyline beyond.
2. Turn left and walk along the Ridgeway for nearly 2 miles, passing two lots of farm buildings. Look for an area of grass with a signpost for crossing footpaths.
3. Turn left here keeping to the hedge on the right at first, then left. Going downhill, Ashbury church is ahead. At the bottom, turn left then bear right round the churchyard of St Marks, *(an interesting church with a Norman doorway)*. From the church continue down the path to the road at the Rose and Crown. Cross the road and turn down the road signposted to Village Hall and Shrivenham.
4. At Manor Farm, where the road turns right, turn left. At the Berrycroft sign, go to the left of the house called "The Shieling". Opposite the last house go over the stile in the corner and follow an enclosed path to the stile into a field. Walk along the edge of this field with the hedge on the right, one field away from the road. Go over the stile in the corner, cross the track and another two stiles, then walk along the next field with the fence on the left, still parallel with the road. At the end of this field, cross a track which goes to the farm on the left, and into another field in which the fence should be kept on the left.

   At the end of this field the path drops to a bridge over a stream with a stile each side. Now head for the electricity pole and a stile beside a gate. Cross the lane and go through the yard of Lower Idstone Farm.

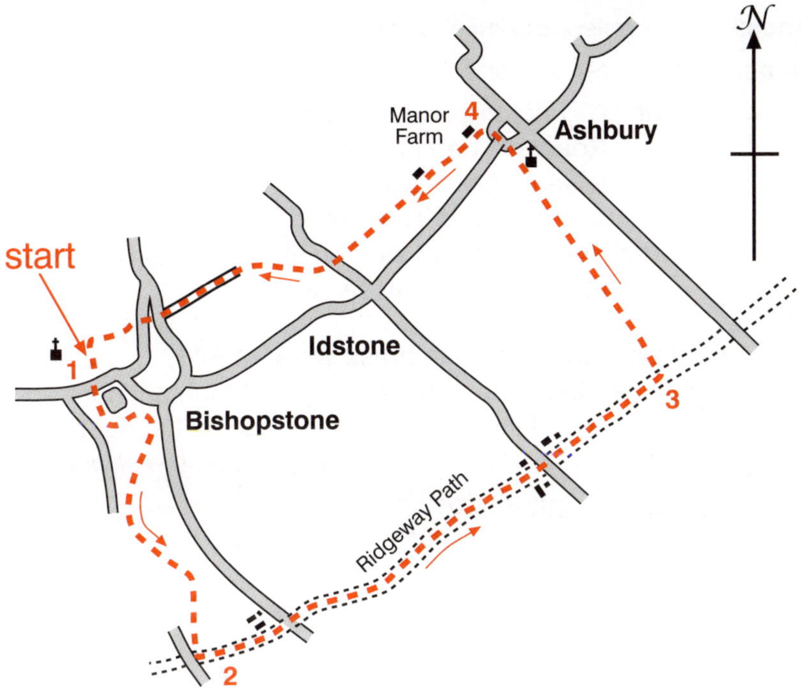

Keep to the right of the horse chestnut tree to a metal stile. Now walk straight ahead, keeping the hedge on the right, to the corner where there are two gates and a footbridge.

In the next field keep the hedge on the left and go ahead into a long green lane. At the road go diagonally left to a stile beside a large willow tree. Cross this field to a stile beside a metal gate. Turn right to road junction, then left into Cues Lane and past Laurel Cottage with straw ducks on the roof.

Where road turns left, go straight ahead passing a thatched house on right, down to and across the first footbridge, then up to the road. Turn left to Bishopstone church *(see stained glass window depicting Wiltshire landscape)* and round the churchyard on a gravel path to a gate. This path leads to the road: turn left for the pond.

Refreshments: Public houses in Bishopstone and Ashbury.

Walk 7 Liddington Hill & Downs

Undulating downland scenery with lovely views. No stiles.

Distance: 5½ miles; 6½ miles including circuit of hill fort

OS Maps: Explorer 157 and 170;Landranger 174

Start:
Car: At juncton of B4192 and Ridgeway Road (SU216805) Roadside parking - from Swindon, turn right off B4192 towards Chiseldon and immediately look for parking on either side of the road.
Bus: Nos. 46 and 48 stop on the B4192 at Ridgeway cross roads *(no Sunday service)*.

Directions:

1. Walk away from Swindon along grass verge of B4192, cross to the bridle gate at the other side of the road, go through and turn right. Walk along the edge of the field, with the fence on the right. *(The first objective can be seen, which is the small peak on the skyline.)*
2. Go through several gates, closing any that have been opened, and continue to the peak. *This was the site of a long barrow but little can be seen of it now.* Keep along the path ahead, still with the fence on the right. *(Although the M4 motorway can be seen to the left, the prevailing wind usually carries the sound away.)* After a mile or so, three galvanised metal gates will be seen.

Liddington Hill

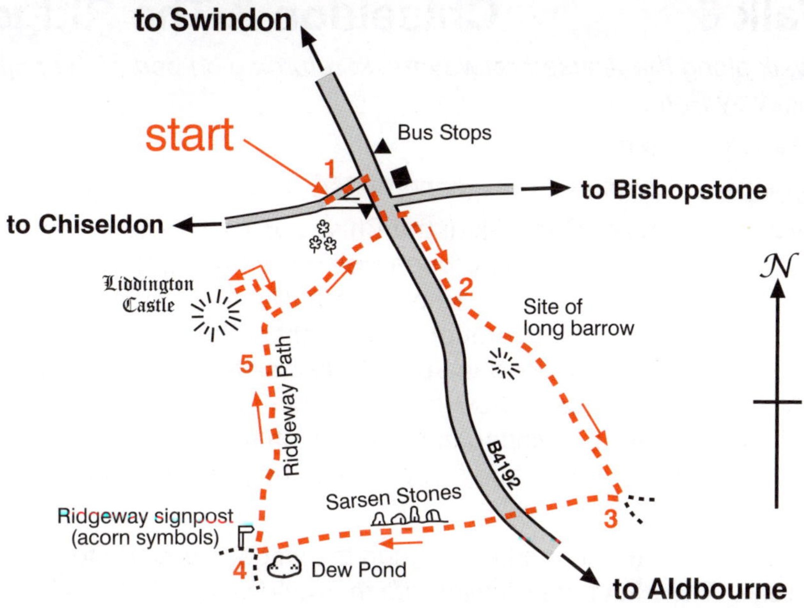

3. Go through the bridle gate, turn right, go through a larger gate and descend the hillside to the road. Cross to the byway opposite and walk along the valley, passing some sarsen stones. *Their natural colour is brown but these are covered with grey lichen.* The track rises and bears left away from the fence. Near the top, on the left, is an ancient dewpond which is now dry.
4. At the junction of paths at the top, turn sharp right on to the Ridgeway Long Distance Path, with the acorn logo. *(The old Ridgeway from Draycot to Foxhill is metalled so an alternative route for walkers was found.)* Ahead, left, can be seen the 'V' formed by the ditch and banks of the Iron Age hillfort, Liddington Castle. After a gate, the path rises gently, with views to both the left and right.
5. It later runs in the middle of a field and curves right to a gateway with a signpost. From here it is possible to take a permissive path to Liddington Castle and walk around the perimeter of this hillfort *(there are wonderful views over Swindon from here)*. Return to the Ridgeway Path and continue downhill while taking in the distant views over the Lambourn Downs. Just after passing the clump of trees which are such a feature of the hill and a Second World War lookout post on the left, the path descends to the road and the start of this walk.

Refreshments: None.

Walk 8 Chiseldon & The Ridgeway

A walk along the disused railway track, returning on part of the higher Ridgeway Path.

Distance: 6 miles

OS Maps: Explorer 157 Landranger 173 & 174

Start: **Car:** Car park at the Chiseldon end of the Chiseldon to Marlborough Railway Path (SU192793). From Junction 15 of the M4 take the A346 towards Marlborough. Turn right at the minor crossroads beyond the petrol filling station in Chiseldon. The car park is on the left past the farm shop.

Bus: Swindon to Marlborough services 70 and X5 *(Mon to Sat)* and 5 *(Sun)* near the petrol station.

Directions:

1. Cross the car park and go through the wooden gate on to the railway path. The path runs parallel with the A346 which is one field away to the left. *Beyond the road the land rises to a ridge on the skyline which will be walked on later. The Swindon, Marlborough & Andover Railway was opened in 1881. It later became part of the Midland & South West Junction Railway. The line was closed in 1961.*
2. After about a mile the track bears left to go round the gypsy camp that is behind the bank on the right. Go through the clump of Scots pines and control barriers to the tarmac road and turn right. After 40 yards turn left through the barriers and continue walking along the railway path for another ⅔ mile when the path dips down to a concrete track with a derelict brick bridge on the right.
3. Turn left to the main road and cross it carefully – the traffic is very fast here. Turn right and walk along the grass verge, passing the double gates across a drive. After another 60 yards along the verge climb up the grass bank on to the tarmac track and walk up the hill towards the radio mast. When the track ends continue along the grass track (the Long Distance Ridgeway Path) with a low grey structure on the right.
4. Turn left and follow the wide mud track (firm after dry weather but can be puddly in the winter) until coming to a wooden sign post at a T-junction; ignore the grass track which goes off diagonally to the left. *At this point look down to the left and see the traffic going along the main road and also where the Railway Path runs between the hedgerows beyond the road.*

5. At the T-junction turn right and then left, following the Ridgeway sign, and continue until the path forks. Take the left fork and go on until seeing a gate across the path. 10 yards before the gate there is a stile on the left. Climb over this stile and walk down the hill, keeping the fence on the right. About halfway down the field go through the gate on the right *(remember how it unfastened so that it can done up again!)*. A broad grass track lies ahead, keeping near the fence for about 100 yards or so and then bearing left down the hillside until it runs parallel with a fence and hedge on the left. *After passing through a gate look up to the skyline half right ahead and the Iron Age Hill Fort of Liddington Castle with its bank and ditch formation will be seen.*
6. Follow the track (ignoring an entry in to a field on the right) which becomes a tarmac road as it bears right. Keep on this road to a T-junction and turn left to continue to the A346 road. The car park is across the road on the left.

Refreshments: Three Trees Farm Shop, adjacent to car park *(not open Mondays and Tuesdays)*.

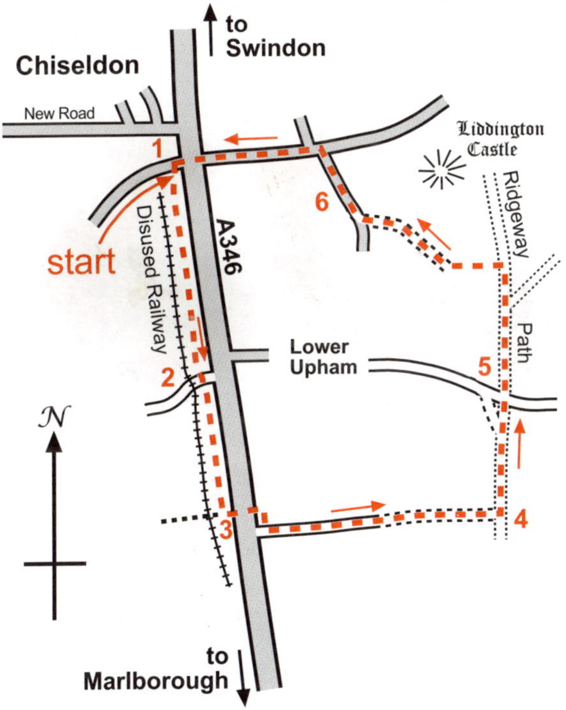

Map reproduced by permission of Ordnance Survey on behalf of The Controller of Her Majesty's Stationery Office © Crown copyright. Licence No. 100033886

Walk 9 — Upper Upham

A downland walk in the area of the medieval villages of Snap and Upham. Good tracks, extensive views and a feeling of isolation.

Distance: 3½ or 6 miles

OS Maps: Explorer 157 Landranger 174

Start: **Car:** Turn off Swindon to Aldbourne road (B4192) on road to Upper Upham and follow road to beyond the semicircle of house on left. Park considerately near the cylindrical storage tank. (SU225772).

Bus: none.

Directions:

1. At the end of the concrete path, and with a barn on the right, continue forward on the track across the valley bottom and up to the hedgerow on the skyline.
2. As the Ridgeway long distance path joins from the right, continue for 20 metres and turn left, still on the Ridgeway. Continue until a track crosses the Ridgeway, with a concrete tank and a radio mast visible on the right. Turn left.

Upham Court

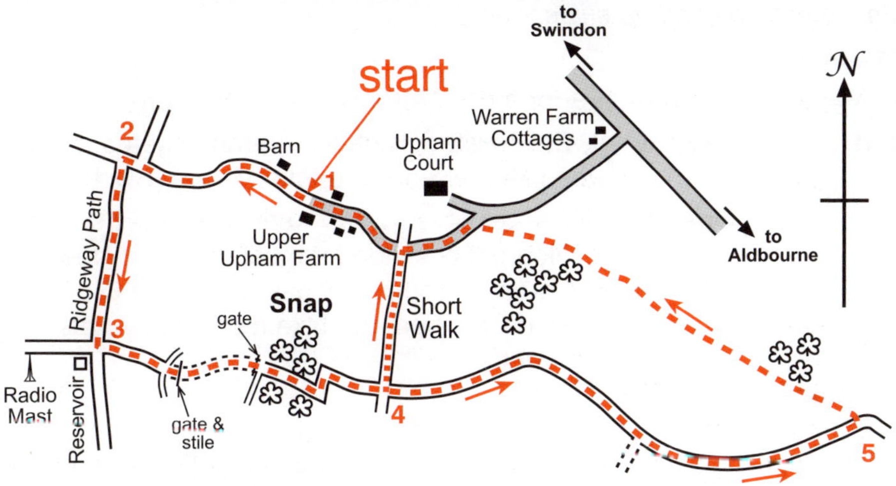

3. Follow this track and, as it turns right, go forward, cross a stile or go through a gate by a wide, metal farm gate. Follow the remnants of a stony path which bears left towards the valley, then veers right and goes through a gateway to follow a path down hill between trees. It eventually turns left, then right and comes to a track junction at a field corner.

4. For the **SHORTER WALK**, turn left and climb to the tarmac road and turn left back to the car.

   For the **LONGER WALK**, carry straight on along the track through the valley. Just after the wood it is possible to walk at the foot of High Clear Down and join the track again near an information board. Continue almost to the main road, and then turn sharp left at a path junction.

5. Follow this path through a gate near the remains of a barn. Keep the hedge on the left until the path veers right to pass close to a clump of trees over a long barrow. Go through the gate and on through another. Pass another clump of trees and go through the next gate. Veer slightly left across a large pasture to reach the gate into a fenced strip of land at the end of which is the road. Turn left to return to the start.

Refreshments: None.

Walk 10 Old Town Green Spaces

An easy walk around Old Town, mainly on firm paths (uneven in places) with a few steps and no stiles.

Distance: 4 miles

OS Maps: Explorer 169 (or a good street map of Swindon).

Start: High Street, Old Town, outside the entrance gates to The Lawn (between Horder and Charlotte Mews) (SU 158837).

Bus: Readily accessible by bus – several routes serve Old Town. Nearest bus stop for most services: Newport Street Co-op. If coming by car use one of Old Town's car parks (££). There are bike racks for cyclists in Wood Street.

Directions:

1. Enter the Lawn. At the end of the tree-lined avenue, turn right and keep right, joining a tarmac surface at the end of The Planks and going downhill. Where the cycle path begins to go uphill again, bear left on to a narrower path. Follow this path beside a lake, keeping it on your left. Go ahead to find a second lake and, at the end of this, turn right. This path, with grass on the right, emerges on to a small open space; cross the cycle path and continue on to a narrower path towards a row of houses. Go ahead, keeping these houses on your left, and enter Bruddel Wood beside house no.23. Follow the Millennium Trail, near the left edge of the wood, up some steps, and across a small road to continue through the wood and emerge on to Marlborough Road.
2. Turn right and cross the road at the pelican crossing. Keeping right, cross Pipers Way with care, then Marlborough Lane. Walk up the grass mound ahead of you and cross the bridge. *You are now on the route of the former Midland & South West Junction Railway.* Follow the path between the houses. Beyond the parking

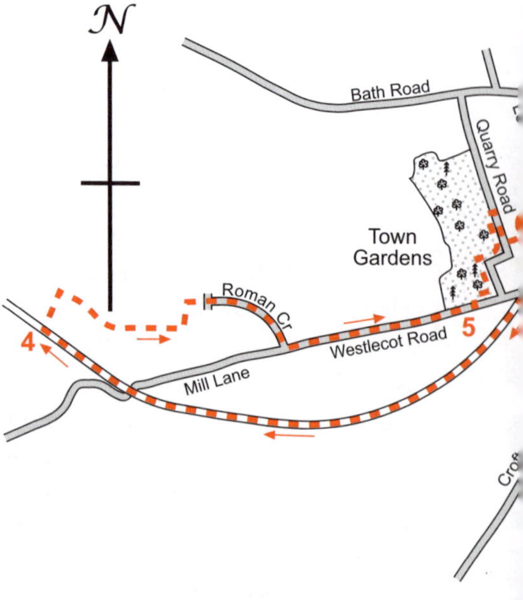

Map reproduced by permission of Ordn
Her Majesty's Stationery Office © Crow

area, turn left along a road, right at a T junction, then left towards an industrial estate where Swindon Junction station used to be. Walk through the estate to find a fenced path in the far-right hand corner. *This is the start of the Old Town Railway Path.*

3. After passing through two short tunnels, look for an information board on the right *about the site of special scientific interest*. The path later emerges from the cutting with views over Wichelstowe to the downs above Wroughton. About a mile after the tunnels, after crossing two minor roads and passing an isolated house on the left, a path joins from the right.

4. Follow this path as it winds uphill. On reaching a level stretch of road, turn right (at house no 36), then ascend a short flight of steps on your left. Follow the tarmac path beside the grass area in front of 20-25 Galen View, then between fences into the end of a cul-de-sac (Roman Crescent). Continue to the T-junction and turn left. Carry on until you reach the entrance to Town Gardens on your left.

5. Enter the gardens, *which were laid out in Victorian times on the site of an old quarry. If you wish, take time to explore the gardens.* To continue the walk from the entrance gates, turn right, pass the aviary, and continue around the perimeter path to the next gate, exiting opposite house no. 32. Turn right and take the narrow alleyway on your left beside no. 27, which runs around the back of Lethbridge Primary School.

6. Turn right and continue along Lethbridge Road. Cross Devizes Road at the pelican crossing, then turn left and cross Newport Street at the next crossing. Turn right and continue past the Co-op store to get back to where you started. Note the blue plaque on the wall as you pass the petrol station.

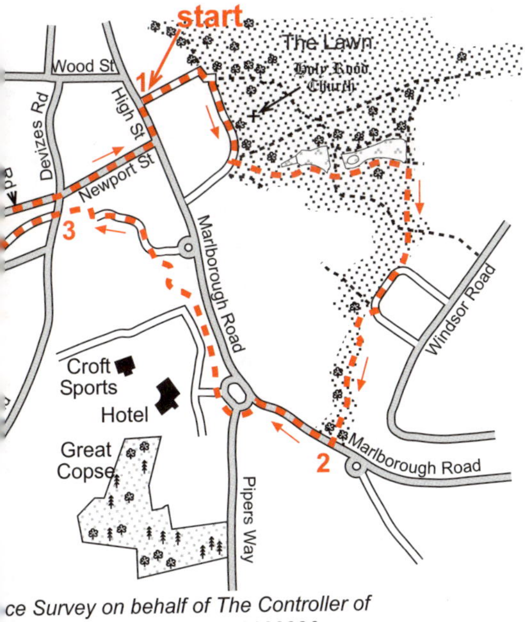

ce Survey on behalf of The Controller of
copyright. Licence No. 100033886

Refreshments:

Pubs and cafes in Old Town.
Kiosk in Town Gardens.

Toilets:

Town Gardens (closed from 1 November to end February).

Walk 11 Downs & Og Valley

A steep climb on to the downs, then mostly easy walking on lanes and good tracks.

Distance: 6½ or 7 miles

OS Maps: Explorer 157 Landranger 173 and 174

Start: **Car:** In car park for railway path, just east of Ogbourne St George (SU204740). By car from Swindon, leave the A346 to Marlborough by the slip road just past the golf course. Go straight over the cross roads towards Bytham Farm and park in the little car park just opposite the road on the left.

Bus: Swindon to Marlborough services 70 *(Mon to Sat)* and 5 *(Sun)* stop in the village.

Directions:

1. Walk out of the car park and up the road ahead. The track climbs slowly at first, passes a path going off to the left, then bends right to climb steeply. At the top of the hill go forward after a track joins from the right and then cross another track. *The Ridgeway long distance path has been left now.* Follow this track for about 1 mile to a junction of tracks at Whiteshard Bottom.
2. Take a sharp turn right on to a rising tarmac lane. Follow this for about 1½ miles - *it is tarmaced in parts and often there is a farm track*

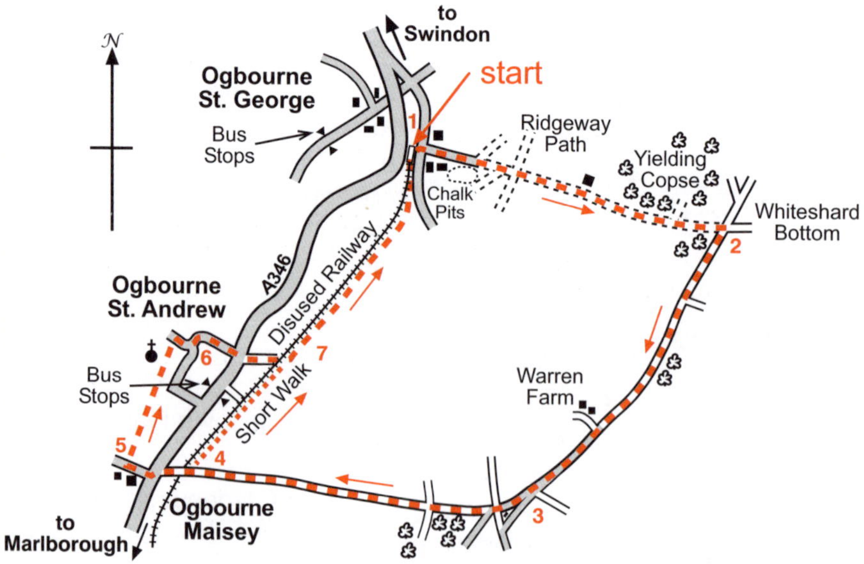

Leaving Ogbourne Maisey

running alongside. Pass Warren Farm on the left and go through a farm complex of silos and storage barns to arrive at a 5-way junction.

3. Take the second track on the right (signed Marlborough), soon passing a wood on the left. Continue on this track for a further 1½ miles until a bridge over the disused railway line is reached. Follow this track down to a junction.

4. For the **SHORTER WALK**, turn right and then left on to the railway path and follow this back to the start.

   For the **LONGER WALK**, turn left and cross the busy A346 (**take great care**), go down the Ogbourne Maisey/Rockley road, over the River Og, and past the early C17 manor house to reach a signed footpath just before a thatched cottage.

5. Pass through the kissing gate and go straight across the field to a stile in the hedgerow. From here, aim for the tree with the church behind it and then follow on with the hedge on the left. Cross the stile and track and walk through the churchyard of St Andrew's church *(notice how flint has been used)*.

6. Turn right on to the road, and then bear left to follow the minor road, with the little River Og beside it, to the A346. Cross carefully and go up a track to reach the railway path. *(The Swindon, Marlborough & Andover Railway was opened in 1881. It later became part of the Midland & South West Junction Railway. The line closed in 1961.)*

7. Turn left just before the dismantled bridge and follow the railway path back to the start. On most of this section there is the choice of walking on the cycle track or the softer bridleway.

Refreshments: Ogbourne St Andrew – Silks on the Downs
Ogbourne St George – The Inn with the Well

Walk 12 Barbury Castle, Smeathe's Ridge & Burderop Down

A delightful downland walk for a clear day.

Distance: 5 miles

OS Maps: Explorer 157 Landranger 173

Start: **Car:** Barbury Castle Country Park (SU157761). From the A4361 at Wroughton or A346 at Chiseldon follow the Country Park signs.

Bus: none.

Directions:

1. Leave the car park by its entrance. At the road, turn right and pass Upper Herdwick Farm on the left.
2. After the farm, take the first gate on the left, signposted for the Ridgeway long distance footpath. Follow the track along an undulating ridge *(Smeathe's Ridge) with fine views - Liddington Castle, Aldbourne Chase, Savernake Forest and the northern edge of Salisbury Plain*. After passing a covered reservoir, enclosed by a fence, the path drops fairly steeply to a gate. At this point join a track with a hedge on both sides that comes in from the left.

Memorial Stone

3. Turn left and follow this track.
4. On joining a concrete track, bear left. Go right off the concrete track and straight ahead keeping a line of trees on the left.
5. At the gate, join a track at the T-junction. Turn left, then bear left at a fork and start to climb Burderop Down. The track skirts to the left of a burial mound and passes the memorial stone to two local writers.
6. At the road, turn left to the car park.

Refreshments: None at time of going to press but planning permission has been given for a café near the toilet block.

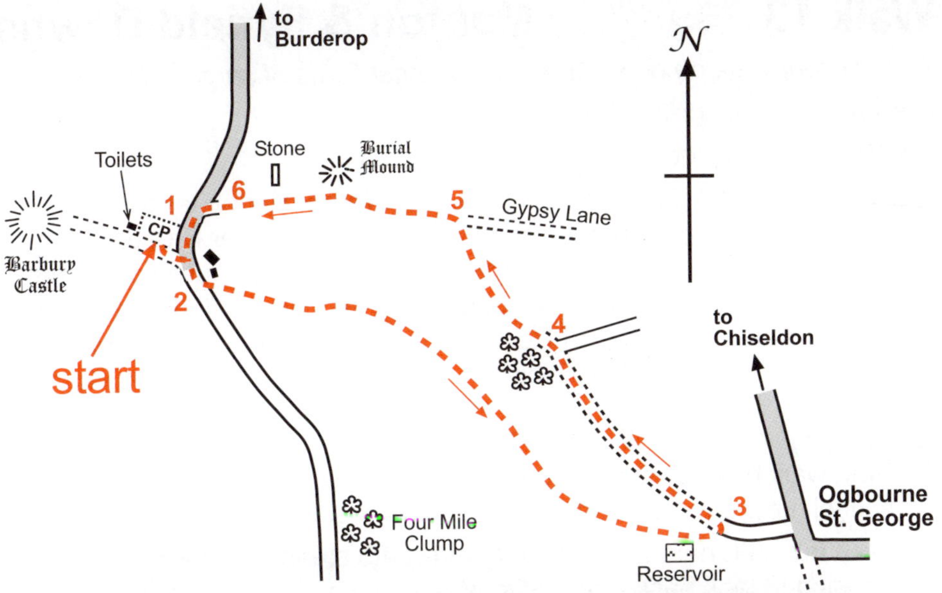

Map reproduced by permission of Ordnance Survey on behalf of The Controller of Her Majesty's Stationery Office © Crown copyright. Licence No. 100033886

Barbury Castle

Walk 13 Manton & Fyfield Downs

An excellent walk on downland and amongst fields of sarsen stones.

Distance: 5½ or 3 miles

OS Maps: Explorer 157 Landranger 173

Start: **Car:** Rockley (SU158719). From Swindon take the A4361 through Wroughton and turn left near Broad Hinton on to road to Marlborough. After about 5 miles, turn right by a telephone box and signpost. Drive into the hamlet of Rockley and park considerately where the road is widest.

Bus: none.

Directions:

1. Start walk by returning through Rockley, passing the one-roomed school, now a restoration workshop, and redundant church.
2. Take the path next to the church and climb steeply to the wood, pausing to look back at the extensive downland views. Keeping the wood on the right, go forward to meet a track at the stables. Continue along this track to the T junction.
3. Turn right and walk for 400 yards keeping a watch for a gap in the fencing on the left.
4. Turn left and cross the gallop, go through a gap in the trees and across another gallop to a tall hedge. With the hedge on the left walk ahead, cross a track and on in the same direction, across "winter gallops" to a hard track.
5. For the **SHORT WALK** turn right and walk towards the reservoir to the track at **10**. Turn right.

For the **LONGER WALK** turn left along the track, passing the private road to the left. Take the right track at a fork for about 100 yards and, keeping the fence on the right, take a grass path to a gate.

6. Go through this gate and follow the track ahead, keeping the fence on the left and ignoring a fork to the right, to reach the valley bottom.
7. Turn right and walk past the firs, after which you can choose a higher or lower route through the Sarsen stone valley. (a) For the higher route, keep the fence immediately on the left and eventually pass through a gate and after a short distance turn sharp right down hill at a fence corner to another gate. Do not go through this gate. (b) For the lower route, continue along the valley bottom with the Sarsen stones and a line of trees on the right. At the end of the line of trees there is a

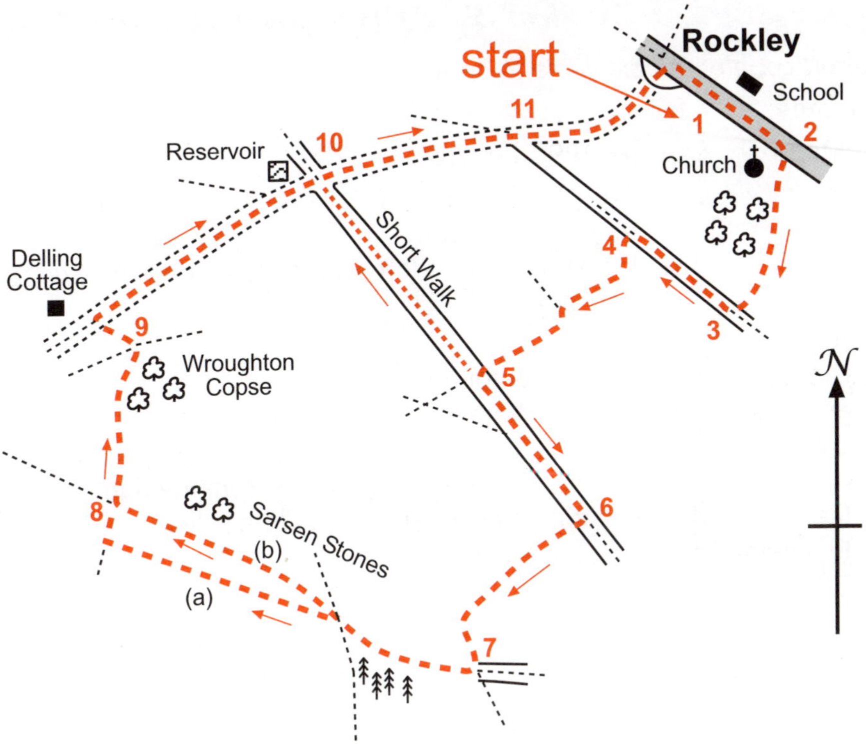

Map reproduced by permission of Ordnance Survey on behalf of The Controller of Her Majesty's Stationery Office © Crown copyright. Licence No. 100033886

fenced area with a gate a short distance up hill on the left. Go through this gate.

8. From the gate, follow the track alongside the fence, keeping the fence and Wroughton Copse on the right. At a fork, bear left and aim towards the cottage amongst the trees (Delling) to a track.
9. Turn right and pass through a gate. Follow the track, out of the nature reserve, to a reservoir.
10. Continue along the track which goes slowly downhill, then more steeply by a beech copse, then rises.
11. At top turn left off the track and follow the edge of the field with the mature beech hedge on the left into Lovers Lane and down to the start.

Refreshments: None.

Walk 14 Wootton Bassett, Little Park Farm & Wilts and Berks Canal

A short country ramble liable to be wet in winter.

Distance: 4 miles

OS Maps: Explorer 169 Landranger 173

Start: **Car:** Park considerately in Cloatley Crescent opposite the end of New Road.

Bus: No 31 from Swindon serves New Road *(no Sunday service)*.

Directions:

1. Cross the railway by the footbridge, turn to the right along a track and fork left almost immediately towards some farm buildings. At the gateway across the track, turn left, over a stile and cross the field, passing between the second and third houses from the right. Cross the road and go straight on between houses to a stile at entrance to a field. Follow the left edge of the field to a footbridge over the Brinkworth Brook and go across.
2. Turn to the right to follow the bank of the brook. At the sharp right bend in the stream go straight on to a gate in the hedge. Go through this gate and on in the same line to a stile in the far hedge. Pass over this stile onto the road, turn left and immediately right through the edge on the far side, over a stile to the next field. Go through the strip of young trees, over a stile and aim slightly left to head for a prominent willow tree beside a pond. Go through the gate behind this pond and cross the field, keeping parallel with the left hedge, to a gap in the far hedge. Go through to a gate by the farm drive.
3. Turn right along the drive to the road. Cross and follow this drive to "Little Park", round the sharp left corner at the end of the walled garden, and turn right to go across a bridge then through a break in the trees. Continue uphill following the line of fence to cross the fence in the hedgerow. This leads to Wootton Bassett Golf Course. *(At this point the line of the old Wootton Bassett to Bath coaching road is joined.)*
4. Continue ahead for 15 metres, through a very thick hedge (where the path used to run) and turn right on the path alongside the golf course. Be alert and considerate along here. Continue along this path, keeping the hedge on the right, go around the 16th tee and bear right over a bridge and go towards the course maintenance building, in front of which is a grass mound with a fence on top.Turn left (to keep

the mound on the right) and continuing to keep the hedge to the right travel downhill to a stile. Cross over this stile and aim to the right of the church tower to reach a stile in the far hedge (with a public footpath sign) and go over it onto a road.

5. Turn left along this road and go through the first gate on the right. (At this point the walk stops using rights of way). Follow the hedge on the left, passing under a mature oak tree, and carry on nearly to the end of the field. *(This is the line of the aqueduct of the Wilts & Berks Canal which was opened in 1810 and closed in 1906.)* Go left through a small metal gate and climb the bank of the old canal. Turn right on the old towpath, then left at a convenient point to cross the bed of the old canal. Climb the far bank and then drop down to the field on the far side. Turn right and follow the field edge. Just before the end of the field, pass through a wide gap in the hedge and carry on to join a farm track.

6. Turn left and follow the track past old farm buildings to rejoin the track used at the start of the walk.

Wootton Bassett Town Hall

Refreshments:

None on route but pubs and cafés in Wootton Bassett

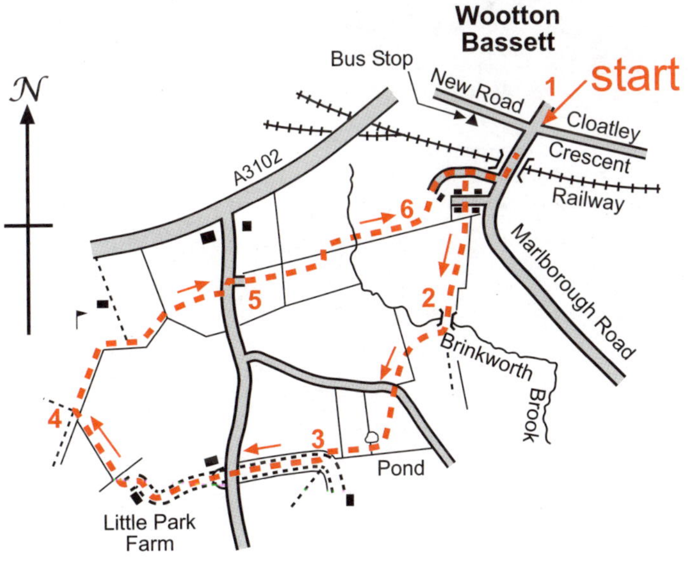

Walk 15 Clouts Wood & Elcombe

A varied walk including woodland and fields.

Distance: 5½ or 3 miles

OS Maps: Explorer 169 Landranger 173

Start: **Car:** Ellendune car park, Wroughton (SU145806), off A4361.

Bus: No. 72 from Swindon to High Street, Wroughton.

Directions:

1. From the car park pass Ellendune Centre on the left, to reach the main road. Go across via the bollards and, keeping to the right of the trees, go across the next road to the pavement by the church hall (former school). Turn left here and follow the road (Priors Hill) round and up.
2. Next to No 82 Priors Hill turn right, where the signpost says 'Clouts Wood' after the last house, and keep the hedge on the right. Follow the hedge round to the corner and now through the gate and turn right. Keeping the mesh fence on the left, go through a gate at the end of the fence and continue with an old fence on the right. At the next corner go ahead over a gate overlooking a little valley, then diagonally left to valley bottom, and up diagonally right to a gate on the left. *This is the entrance to Clouts Wood Nature Reserve maintained by Wiltshire Wildlife Trust.* Keep going straight ahead ignoring any paths to right or left and at the end go down steps curving to the right.

Clouts Wood

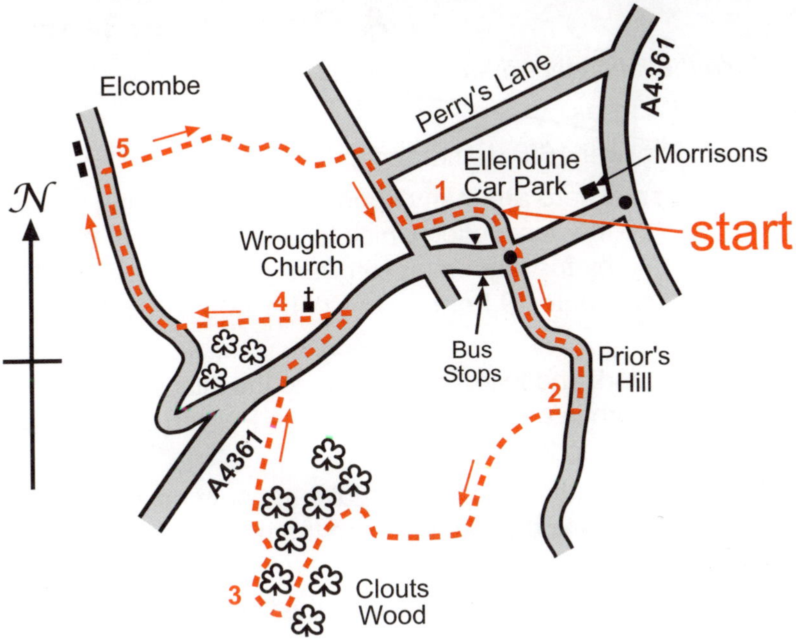

3. Beyond the steps, keep the wooded hillside on the right and when the wire fence is reached turn right. Coming to a gate in the fence on the left, turn right, go up some steps and then turn left. Just after the WWT notice board, turn left down some steps to the fence again, then turn right to follow the path to a footbridge. Go through the gate and turn left to follow the path, then turn right through a small wooded area keeping mainly to the left, to a gate with a hedge on the right which is followed to the road. Turn right here along the grass verge. Where the road bends, carefully cross the road and turn left to Wroughton church.
4. Take the asphalt path which heads through a gate and downhill to Elcombe. Turn right here, passing Elcombe Hall Farm on the right.
5. Go through the first gate on the right and ahead across this long field to a low stile between two large trees. Cross the second field keeping the fence on the right over a footbridge and stile in the corner. In this third field, angle diagonally left aiming for a telegraph pole on the other side of the hedge where there is a gate. In the next field, go across to the right hand corner and between two houses. Turn right along the road, then left along Elcombe Avenue to Wharf Road. Turn right to a signpost to Ellendune and the start.

Refreshments: Only in Wroughton

Walk 16

Peatmoor, Shaw & River Ray Parkway

A walk within the landscaped areas of West Swindon.

Distance: 3½ miles

OS Maps: Explorer 169 Landranger 173

Start: **Car:** There are many opportunities for starting this walk but the description which follows starts from the car park by the lagoon just off Peatmoor Way (SU115863).

Bus: Route 19 from Town Centre stops nearby *(see map)*.

Directions:

1. Leave the car park and follow the lagoon to the inlet stream at its western end. Turn left, cross the road at the Pelican crossing and follow the footpath to 2 on map.
2. At the junction of paths, turn left and take the path past the school. Cross the road, keeping Shaw Farm on the right, until reaching Old Shaw Lane.
3. Turn left and walk up the lane. Keep to the line of the original Shaw lane by bearing right, then following Shaw Road, then leaving it again by turning right after crossing Ridge Green. This is now a cycle track which is followed until through the subway under Whitehill Way.
4. Continue past a children's playground then through another subway with a stream below. Continue forward with the stream and woodland on the left, industrial buildings on the right.
5. Where paths cross, turn left on to the route of the disused Moredon Railway line which runs between two hedges. *(The Moredon Railway formed part of the Midland & South West Junction Railway that was opened in 1884 and closed in 1961.)* Follow this track until

Peatmoor Lagoon

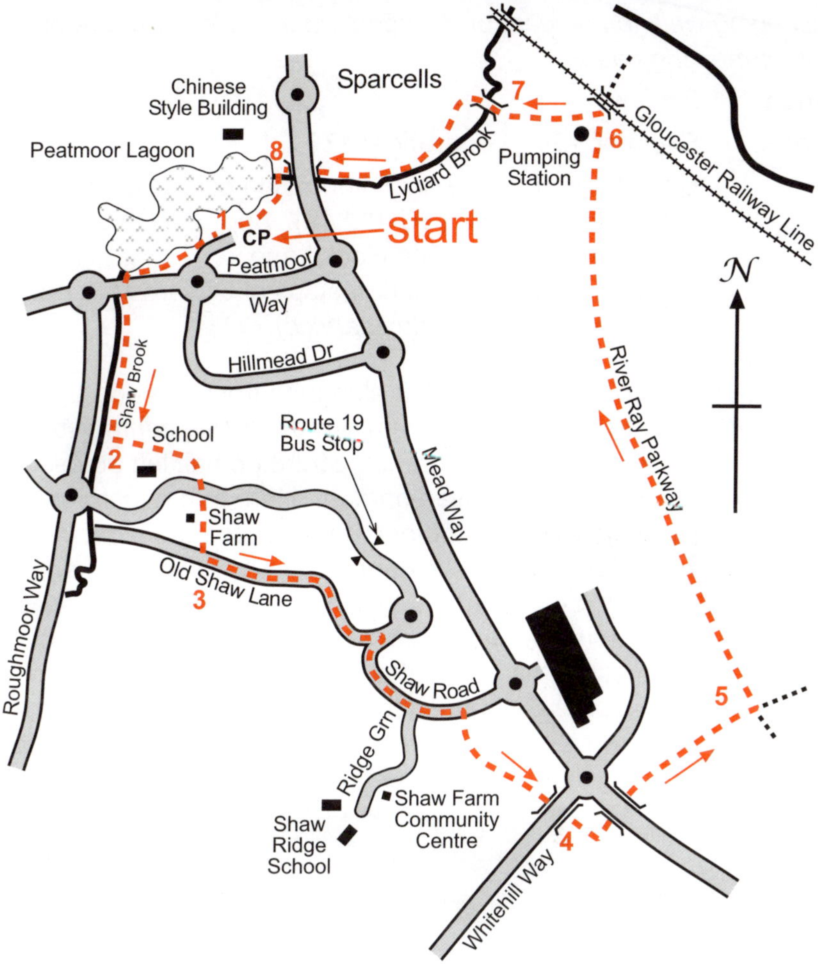

just before the brick bridge.

6. Turn left between a circular building (pumping station) and the Gloucester railway line (active) and follow this path to Lydiard Brook.
7. Turn left and walk on a tarmac path between the stream, on the left, and some houses. This will lead through a subway to face a Chinese style building.
8. Immediately turn left, then right and follow the edge of Peatmoor Lagoon *(built as a flood lagoon, wildlife habitat and recreation area in 1986)* until reaching the car park from which the walk started.

Refreshments: None directly on the route

Walk 17 Lydiard Park & Purton

A challenging walk to the west of Swindon. Many stiles and a good chance of meeting cattle.

Distance: 5 miles

OS Maps: Explorer 169 Landranger 173

Start: **Car:** From the cafe and information centre in Lydiard Country Park (SU102846). Approach through Whitehill Way and Hook Lane.

Bus: No. 53 from Swindon stops at Lydiard Millicent church *(no Sunday service)*.

Directions:

1. With your back to the cafe, turn left along the track passing Lydiard House *(the home of the St. John family with its 18th century facade)* on the right. Just past the conference centre go half left across a small car park to the corner of a walled garden. Here turn right for a few yards to go through a gate in the perimeter fence. *(Looking back to the right St. Mary's, the 13th century parish church of Lydiard Tregoze with many 17th century monuments to the St. John family, can be seen.)* Go forward with a hedge on the left for 200 yards, ignoring a gap, to a pair of stiles almost at the end of the field. Over the stiles and a ditch, go half right to a new stile in the hedge. Keep on the same line, across the line of the new oil pipeline, past the corner of a hedge with houses beyond, and along it to a stile at the road.

Lydiard Mansion

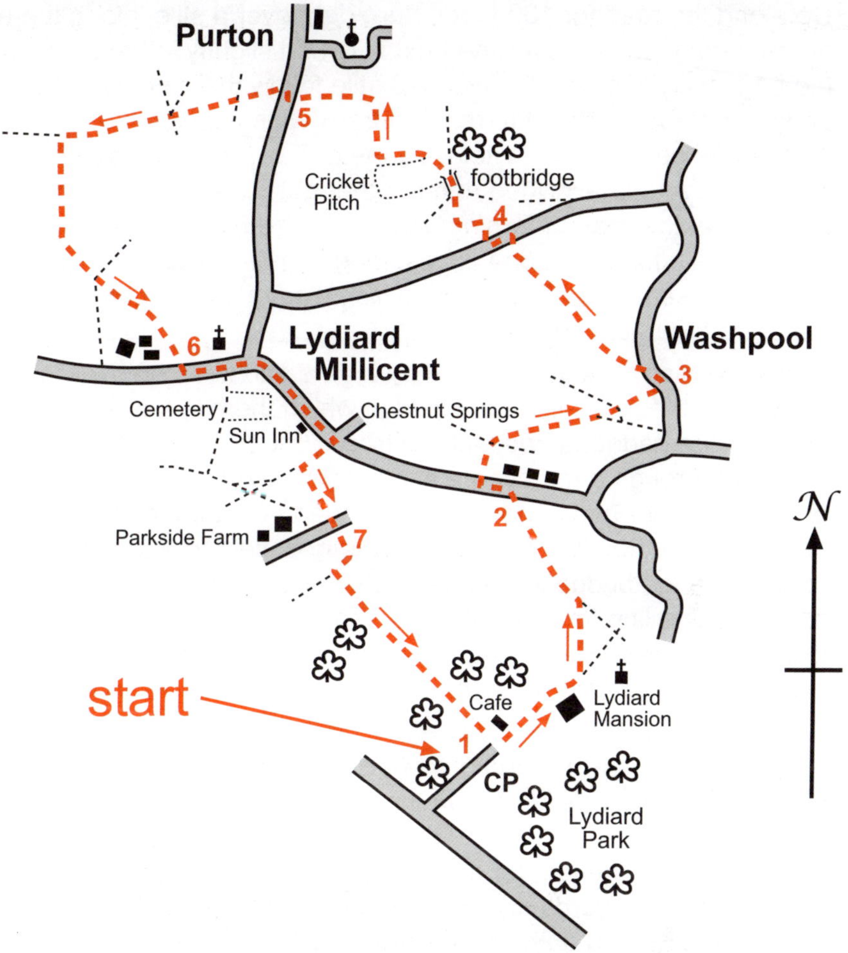

2. Cross the road (take care - it carries a lot of traffic) and turn left past a group of houses (Holborn). Just past the last house, turn right into a driveway, then slightly left through a gate and along a trodden path past stables to come out into a field with a stream on the left. Keep on to a stile and in the next field veer gradually away from the hedge and stream, to a stile to right of the conifer hedge ahead. Cross the tarmac drive, go over the stile opposite, through a paddock with hedge on the right, to a stile. In the next field go half left to a stile near the white house, over this and turn left.
3. This is Washpool. Go along the road for 100 yards, left up a track for 400 yards, then over a stile and half left to a metal stile in the hedge ahead. Cross the next field on the same line to another stile in the left hand field edge. Here go right along the track to the road (Stone Lane).

4. Go along the road for 100 yards, turn right over a stile, along the edge of the garden centre, over the next stile and slightly left to a stile at the beginning of a wood. Over this stile follow the path over a sleeper bridge and soon turn left to reach a track which goes left along the northern edge of a cricket field. At the end of the field, go through a gate, through a small wood and another gate, then through the field to a gate at the road. *(Turning right along the road, a fine stone barn and Purton church in a beautiful setting can be seen. Nearby is Purton Manor House (no public access) which was rebuilt by Lord Chandos at the end of the 16th century.)*

5. Cross the road to go over a stile by a gate and keep on over four stiles, roughly on the same line, to a field in which there is a pylon. Turn left to follow the hedge, across a farm track *(Bagbury Lane Farm is on the right)* through a metal gate and across next field, aiming for the far right corner - aim at poplar trees ahead. Go through the gate here (yellow paint) then half right across the next field to a stile with a white crossbar, a footbridge and another stile. Keep on across the next field on same line to a pair of stiles. Then go half left across the field towards some houses and left through a stile or gap in the fence. At the end of some gardens turn right to follow the fences to the road.

6. *This is Lydiard Millicent.* Turn left along this road to the junction *(church on left is well worth a visit)*. Bear right and follow the road, passing the car dealer and Sun Inn on the right. Go over the roundabout and, opposite Chestnut Springs, go straight up a path, white house on the left, for about 100 yards to the stile. Turn left and go for about 180 yards on a path between hedge and gardens. Go through the kissing gate, across the field, through another kissing gate to a lane.

7. Cross the lane to the stile opposite and follow the hedge on left for about 50 yards. Go over a footbridge then half right to a stile into a plantation of young trees. Turn left - ignore another stile to the right. Keep on over the footbridge, still with a hedge on the left, through an open field, then across another field, eventually on a raised track, through a kissing gate beside a cattle grid. *This is Lydiard Park.* Keep straight on and, at the next junction, turn right, then left alongside the playing fields to the starting point.

Refreshments: In the Visitor Centre at Lydiard Country Park - café or vending machines.
The Sun Inn, Lydiard Millicent

Stanton Park & Stanton Fitzwarren — Walk 18

A varied and interesting walk to the north of Swindon using well-marked paths with views but no real hills.

Distance: 2½ miles. Add 1 mile if travelling by bus.

OS Maps: Explorer 169 Landranger 173

Start: **Car:** Stanton Country Park car park (SU178896). From Swindon, take the A361 towards Highworth; turn left for Stanton Fitzwarren and left at brown sign for the country park.

Bus: No. 7 from Swindon on A361 to Stanton Fitzwarren turning.

Directions:

1. Take the sandy path to the right of the big barn, soon passing some fenced apple trees on the left. *On the right is Stanton House Hotel, with its ha-ha wall to keep livestock off the lawn; beyond is St Leonard's church, partly hidden by trees and on the left is the lake.* Keep on the sandy path, passing a path for the lake and woodland on the left. About 40 metres beyond, take a path on the right, cross a stile and turn right.
2. Walk up the path with trees and bushes on both sides, turning left at the corner of a tall wire fence. After going through a wooden kissing gate turn right to a stile in the stone wall ahead. You are now in Stanton Fitzwarren. Turn right along the road (Trenchard Road) passing the Old Rectory on the right. Where the road bends left, go straight on to visit St Leonard's church, founded in the fourteenth century. *Note the interesting porch and doorway.* Retrace your steps to the road and turn right.
3. Walk along the left side of the road, being wary of traffic, and turn left into The Avenue. At the end of the tarmac continue ahead into a large field *with views of Liddington Hill on the right*, keeping the hedge on the left until you reach a gap between fields on the left. Turn left and walk along the grassy track beside deer fencing to a T junction and turn left. When the fencing ends, turn right into a field *with distant views ahead and right* and walk with hedge/fence on the left to a footpath on the left.
4. Walk down the footpath to Trenchard Road and turn right until reaching Mill Lane on the left. Turn left and, after a left-hand bend, look for cottage called The Mill on the left. *About 25 metres further on, there*

are remains of pedestrian gates where a level crossing on the Swindon & Highworth Light Railway would have been. Ignore the stone track on the left and take the next track on the left, signposted Kingsdown; turn left through a wide gap in the hedge and go across the field, *noting the low stone wall supporting a former railway track*.

5. Resist going on to the railway track (not a right of way) and walk along the edge of the field beside the track to a kissing gate in the corner. Through the gate, turn left and walk 50m to another kissing gate and up

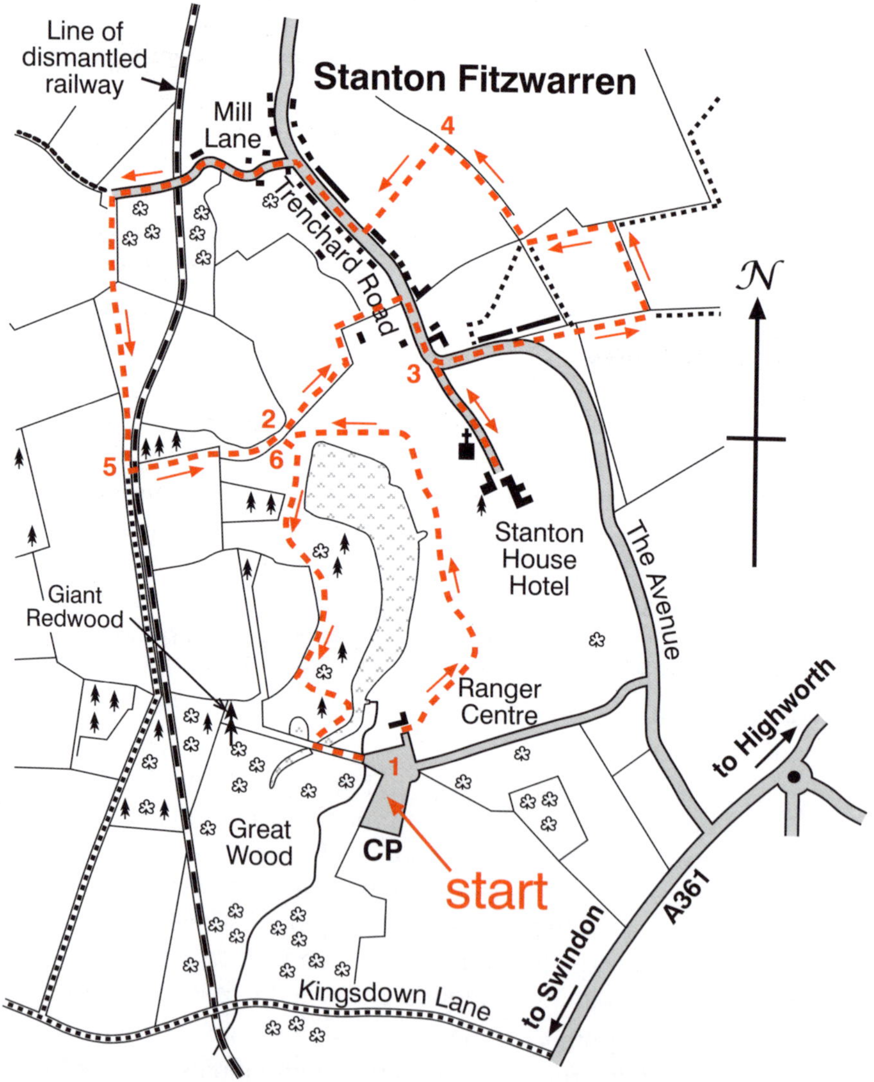

Map reproduced by permission of Ordnance Survey on behalf of The Controller of Her Majesty's Stationery Office © Crown copyright. Licence No. 100033886

Stanton House

steps. Cross the track to a footpath, *noting the stone abutments where there was a low bridge*. Keep to the path through a wooded area until you reach a stile on the right to re-enter Stanton Country Park.

6. At the sandy path turn right, then left at the signpost for Farm Car Park and Woodlands. Ignore path on left (Parkland 250m) and bear right along woodland path. At the next signpost, Car Park 250 m, turn left and walk across a couple of footbridges to a T junction. Turn right and, when you meet a concrete track, turn left to the car park.

Refreshments: At Stanton Park Hotel, accessible opposite the lake.

Toilets: At Ranger Centre

Walk 19 Coate Water & Broome Manor

A walk on the southern edge of Swindon through Coate Water Country Park and around the golf course.

Distance: 4 miles

OS Maps: Explorer 169 Landranger 173

Start: **Car:** Coate Water Country Park car park (SU178827).
Bus: Many bus routes pass the entrance which is off Coate Water roundabout at the junction of Queens Drive, Marlborough Road and Dorcan Way.

Directions:

1. Leave car park and climb up to the dam of the reservoir and turn left to walk alongside the lake which will be on the right. The path leads round the lake and eventually crosses another dam with the nature reserve on the left.
2. Turn right after crossing this dam and follow the path through the woods to reach Broome Manor Lane. Turn right on to the path between the road and the end of the lake until it reaches the point where it meets the path which runs along the western side of the lake.

Coate Water

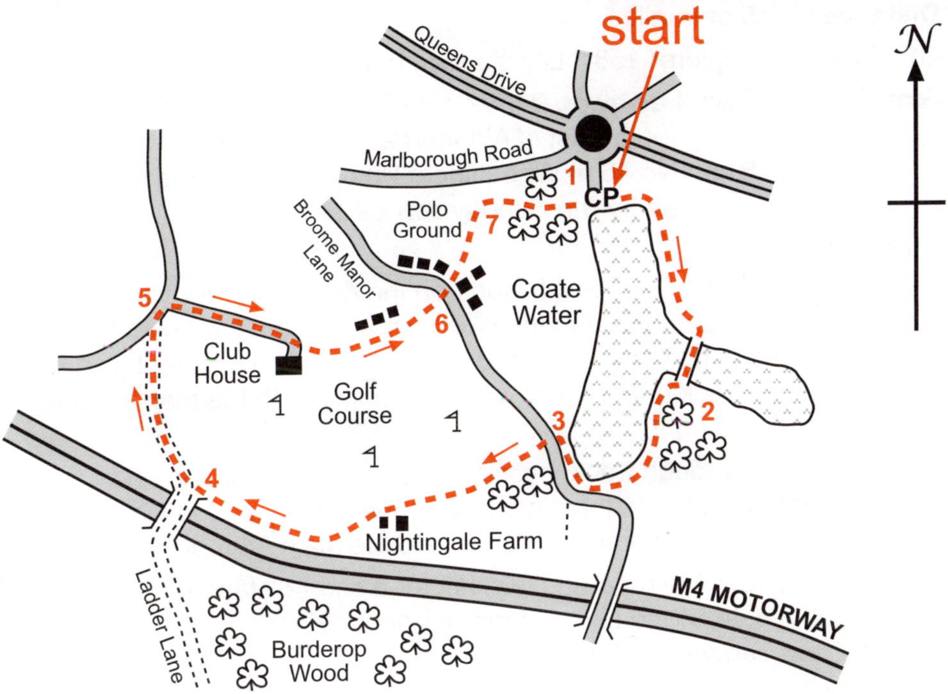

3. Cross the road and follow the path outside the edge of the golf course, past Nightingale Farm, then Fir Clump beside the motorway until a bridge over the motorway.
4. Bear right to follow the track, Ladder Lane, which formed part of the old coaching route to Marlborough, slightly uphill to the road and turn right.
5. At the traffic lights turn right and walk towards the golf course complex. Pass the club house on the right and follow the path with houses on the left and the golf course on the right until it emerges on to Broome Manor Lane.
6. Cross the road and a patch of grass to enter the polo ground. Walk along the lower edge of the polo ground, with trees planted on both sides of the path, until the far corner by a pond. Cross the footbridge over a stream and turn left to get back to the car park.

Refreshments: At Coate Water kiosk, if open, and the Golf Club House.

Walk 20 Chilton Foliat & Hungerford

A walk in the Kennet Valley, crossing rivers and the Kennet & Avon Canal. Well worth the extra travelling distance.

Distance: 5 or 6 miles

OS Maps: Explorer 158 Landranger 174

Start: **Car:** Lay-by on B4192 on edge of Chilton Foliat, 5 miles south-east of Aldbourne (SU316706).

Bus: No.46 at Wheatsheaf Pub just east of the start and lay-by *(no Sunday service)*.

Directions:

1. Walk towards the village with wood on the right. In a few yards, turn right on to footpath through the wood, cross a footbridge over the River Kennet and come to a road. Turn left and walk along this road, ignoring the track to the right, until the junction with the main road is reached. Turn right.
2. Go uphill on a rough track, passing through some wooded and uncultivated land, and then into open country with a good view. Follow the track down past a cottage and on to the main A4 road.
3. Carefully cross the road and turn left for a short distance and go through a gate by the side of farm buildings. Keeping the farm on the left, cross two footbridges over the River Dun. The Kennet & Avon Canal is now reached which is crossed on a wooden swing-bridge at Marsh Lock. Turn left and walk alongside the canal until coming close to Hungerford church.
4. Shortly before the church, cross the canal again by another swing-bridge. Follow the path over two small footbridges, through a hedge and diagonally left up across the field to the main road, A4. Cross the road with care, go through the hedge, up some steps, over a stile and follow the signed path up hill. At the top the path begins to drop and passes the end of an active airstrip with signs alerting walkers to take care. Continue more steeply down hill to the road. Turn right and walk along the footpath.
5. On coming to the Wilts-Berks county sign turn left, cross the River Kennet and reach Leverton (note the cottages on the right) and a road.
6. For the **SHORTER WALK**, turn left here and walk through the village of Chilton Foliat, *noting the public house and church on the right*, until reaching the starting point on the left.

   For the **LONGER WALK**, go straight forward across the road and up a tarmac road past the entrance to Chilton Estate office. At the top of this hill turn left *(opposite the track to Chilton Farms)*, on to a rough track, at first through a wood and then beside a field. When the track dips down, look for a stile on the left, go over it and cross the field diagonally (under the cables) to a stile. Cross the road junction and take the road down hill. At a fork, keep right and later join the road. Turn right and walk through Chilton Foliat (see notes on short walk).

Refreshments: Chilton Foliat - Wheatsheaf
Hungerford - various.

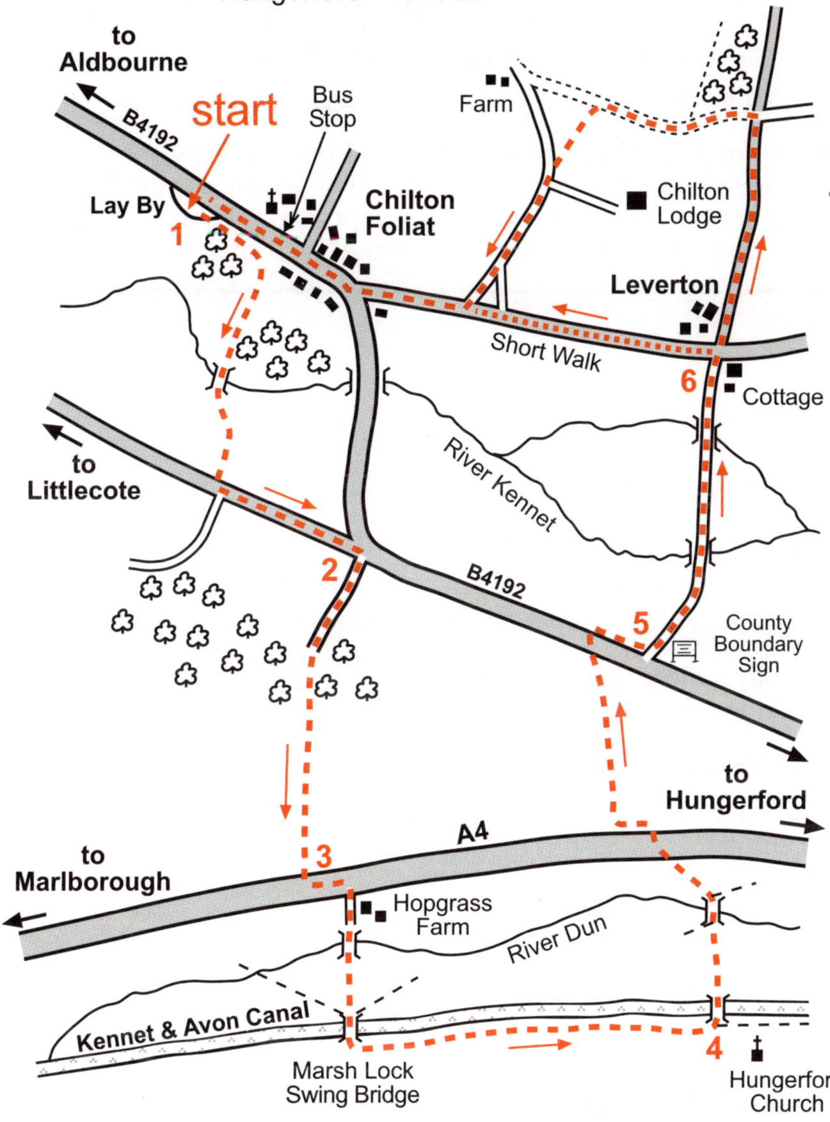

Other books in this series are:

9 Downland Walks

12 Walks around Marlborough

10 Walks from Village Pubs near Swindon

They may be obtained in Swindon from Waterstones and from the Tourist Information Centre (in the library); in Marlborough from The White Horse Bookshop and the craft centre in St Peter's Church.

Problems on Paths

If you find any problems such as damaged stiles, fallen trees or crops growing over paths, please report the exact location to:

Rights of Way Officer, Swindon Borough Council, Civic Offices, Euclid Street, Swindon, SN1 2JH

or email rightsofway@swindon.gov.uk

The information will be passed to the relevant highway authority.